What is Another Word for Intimacy?

by
Amanda Baker

PUBLISHING

Baltimore, Maryland, USA

Library of Congress Control Number: 2022945890
ISBN (paperback): 979-8-9850704-3-9

Cover Art by Alexa Laharty (Instagram @alexaelisabeth).
Interior design by Yellow Arrow Publishing.
For more information, see yellowarrowpublishing.com.

The depths
      dig
          deep
              down.

                                    I dove dangerously.

                    Despite doubt. I devote. . . .

I devote this to

                                              YOU.

Contents

WHAT IS ANOTHER WORD FOR INTIMACY?

Absence.

Tangled wisps of hair
Heads on pillows
Connected particles,
Dreams of tomorrows
Locked between patience
And your
A B S E N C E.

Imagination / Creation.

These feelings won't hesitate / they broke the pause to our ending /
and I can't remember how to spell nervous / so I e x p r e s s / now
you t o u c h / I am filled with / a d m i r a t i o n / an ability to get
in stillness / vibrate in frequency / across highways and counties
/ softens our bodies / crack through inaccessible / no longer
hardened / closed / locked / guarded / I trace your freckles / bound
on the road less traveled / a Bachman's Sparrow flew by / a line of
turtles / and two otters intertwined / I believe we are never alone /

These feelings won't hesitate / so I go back and recreate / a thousand
ways we kiss in torrential rain / trust in Earth's soil / in clouds'
cries / more than foolish leaders / or doctrines and written ethics
/ insecure power in disguise / I let go of power / to be your equal /
transparent / feelings make us people /

These feelings won't hesitate / they bypass greed / envy / doubt
/ betrayal / in reverie / I evince euphoria / and thus my world
follows suit / cease storytelling from without / harp from within /
imagination: secret to creation / f e e l / claim it / it's done / a true
desired state fulfilled / doubt disturbs / the way doubt originally
crushed us / please A N I M A T E sensations to life /

Now with c o n v i c t i o n / we are all we wish

My Love Language Must Be.

after Zane Frederick

It does not matter what my love language is because when I saw you everything changed, and I said:

I would love you in all ways / in all languages / in glances / in touching pinkies / in laughter / in shared music / in different food tastes / in photographs / in notebooks / in empty notebooks / because I wouldn't have to write poems about you / because you would be here / and my poems would write themselves / in shared language / L O V E in a shared space / does not need language at all.

The Fruit Mint Gum Variety Pack.

I am still analyzing a conversation from six weeks ago . . .
like a piece of my own gum stuck on the bottom of my shoe
now everywhere I go . . . I leave a little bit of your residue.
It fades as a broken record memory
where I can't remember if the flavor was peppermint or sugar sweet.
Which must mean that you're not that important
to hold so much of my thinking.
Either way I don't want to waste it
I must make the piece last as long as I can taste it.
Because I fear for when my taste buds burn out of that last hint
and to be truly honest, deep inside, I know it was mint.
A L W A Y S M I N T.

Paper House.

Attachment is a self-destruction
Whereas connection is the evolution
Only a few I've connected
Left with impossible solutions
Only one matters
But how do you know?
A connection is a trust
An attachment is a glue
This paper house still stands
No nails or hammers U S E D.

When I Feel Home.

Home is a place I go to within myself
It has nothing to do with the external world
Sometimes it's a tornado with lots of wind and heaviness
Sometimes it's a sunset with comfort and peacefulness
Sometimes it's a memory that fits into a song
A melody with words that tattoo on my heart
Sometimes it's even the drum
The beating and breathing that sets me apart
A home that lives in both light and dark
A home where there are big rooms and small
Floors filled with nothing and of it all
Sour and sweet
Loud and soft
Fear and trust
Big or tall
If I can't live in these rooms
Then I am no H O M E at all.

**I hope you are healed
Every time your eyelids shut
As yours did for
M I N E.**

Fascination or infatuation.

I choose to follow the thread that lays beyond and underneath /
the thread that tugs at arteries / as I ask questions of phenomena
and parallel beings / paradoxes / and complete wonder / sublime /
I choose to wander this way and that / turn around and view you
from upside down / circle you / gallop / behind / and around /
the shadows look brighter / emotional meters go off the chart / I
choose my fascination in you as A R T / I choose obscure / scribble
names in symbols / whispers / if you ever were here / you'd feel the
irresistible / to choose instead of want / chosen instead of fallen
upon / everything that matters is difficult / we live in answers /
I live in fascination and yet often write as if in disgust / I am not /
let's use our senses / see lust as greatest moments of history instead
of distraction / we let something so beautiful eventually turn to
dissatisfaction / I will not let it / I stay in forward motion / I choose
fascination even if you were never here / you fascinate me without
even being aware.

Stranger.

You became a stranger overnight
My lyrical genius fires when fired
And I'm missing someone I've only seen
I escape in my tornado
Spinning cyclone
Of a scent I never scented
Devised, not smelled
Hypothesized, not spelled
But hypnotized
By my own poison
Nauseating
I still drank it
So I could write this down.
Captivated
Intoxicated
Evaporated
Up to vapors
Of mist
And dew.
Drops
Prepare
But
End at dawn.
The sun isn't up for long.
And all I got was this song.
I'm writing for someone who doesn't exist.
I'm writing for who I think you are.
I'm writing for what I think I am.
I'll never live up to my written self.
We'll never be this crafted story.
My faith in connection
Is restoring.

Please don't be a stranger.
Meet me on our date.
The calendar doesn't lie.
Time is a fragment, only of our mind.
And I'll keep counting
Betting on these signs.
I'm writing for someone who doesn't exist.
I'm writing for who I think you are.
I'm writing for what I think I am.
I'll never live up to my written self.
We'll never be this crafted story.
Please don't be a S T R A N G E R.

I say you can love more than one person.

And 51% of people say, "no, you can't" / they tell me they believe in soulmates / any other person is just a 'before-mate' / and once they find that one true love / they are settled and complete / 'til they become part of the divorce rate / then anyone else is just an 'after-mate' / and I'm none of them.

Love is a verb / love dies from neglect / I say love continues and continues and continues beyond the edges / t r a n s c e n d s / zips and zooms / widens / and curls / to propel / and never possess / we neglect when restricted / and I am freedom.

49% of people say, "oh yes, you can" / and you do / because they know me / and they do, too / many are hiding in their picket fence houses / surrounded by cut grass / work routine / and autopilot / but they do, too / they love in secret / love from a distance / I want to love from only inches.

I say you can love more than one person / so I make it 50/50 / and from everything within me in years to come that number will reach infinity / we love more than one child / our children / stepchildren / adopted children / all the children / and teach them to love each other / in multiple kinds of ways / yet at a certain age . . . we are supposed to stop / to behave / I say you can love more than one person / isn't that G R E A T?

If they see the way they say they see me . . .
then I'd be . . .

the undershirt tucked closest to the heart, the first thing put on and the last taken off / the sugar in coffee or tea, the sweetness stirred and sipped

Oh   so   s l o w l y

Warmth. Only warmth. I'd be only warmth
Melting the freeze over the heart
The medicine needed
The relief in snooze on your alarm
The security blanket
The invitation
And RSVP
The cellular ring
The concert on stage
The only tones in your brain
The hunger
The craving
The style
The smile. Always a smile.
I'd be always a

S M I L E.

Green.

This dress still hangs in my closet / never been too good at giving things away / I also must be stunted in my growth because it still lays gently at my waist / circa 2009 / 4th of Julys hang heavy / the background music still plays / Animal Collective sung on folded chairs / red, white, and blue flags on shirts / the star-spangled banner still rings with embarrassment to its name / celebrate loss in water weight from alcohol / the poison tells us to keep going / gazebo lingers of conversation / just a couple of kids / back porches / mosquito bites / laughter on car tops / ping-pong balls with smiley faces / brainwashed from capitalism / I kept the tags / can I sell it back / the green dress

The green dress picks me
Green dress picks me
Dress picks me
Picks me.
Pick me.
Pick me.
Pick me.
Me.
Me.
M E.

Same Skin.

The browns and hazels / look deeply / feel tantric / I wrote it once /
I must have meant it / stained in footprints / came in as magic /
to wonder what is next / playing safe / or to ask / I'm asking / what is
this feeling / or lack thereof / somehow it's fleeting / to feel our feet
fleet, forging fake fulfillment / or is it something wistful, or more /
out of a shell / or in it / longing in the same skin / longing in the
same S K I N.

Take me to the mountains.

I shout, "take me to the mountains," / but don't fall in love with
the idea / I heard poets are good at that / envisioning finish lines
before "on your mark, get set, go" is even comprehended / and
the mountains froze like glaciers to then only melt with global
warming / instead get on a plane / a one-way ticket to anywhere
/ close your eyes and pick a spot on a map / or spin the globe and see
where it lands / the middle of the water / the Bermuda Triangle /
sounds exhilarating / looking from any angle / you can't lose / it
can suck me in / make me dizzy / embarrass myself / leave 50 cups
out / alone / once I'm down at the bottom / mysteriously vanished
/ independent / taken away / when I shouted take me to the
mountains. . . . I meant water / so please don't say okay.

I shout, "take me to the mountains," / but don't fall in love with
the idea / I heard poets are good at that / envisioning finish lines
before "on your mark, get set, go" is even comprehended / because
now all of the sudden I smell like you, and we haven't even bypassed
so much as being six feet apart / how did mountains turn into time
travel / sleepovers / late night tickles / laughter / / or what you do
when I embarrass you / because I tend do that / or leave my cups all
over the place / and how do I know you won't turn away? / how can
I? / when all I did was shout take me to the mountains and you said
O K A Y. . . .

Leave Me in Your Pocket.

It was a pocket / a place for small candy / a wallet / keys to places I never got to know / new candy I'll never get to taste / even though you invited me in / the pocket at that time was filled with other things / a speck of dust / hot air / W O R D S / T I C K I N G / S T I L L N E S S / I watched it / I replayed it / R E W I N D / yet it's different / once I left the pocket / returned to the ground / felt the dirt in my toes / new words came / we unfroze / and the message changed / like all that existed in the pocket was only welcome in the pocket / I know you turned yours inside out / and I know you can't get it back either / I never put anything in my pockets / I don't invite anyone in / because I don't want to turn mine inside out / looking for something that no one believes to exist.

Okay so maybe I invite you in my pocket . . . because in a few hours I realized that it's not openness or willingness that's so painful / it's the rejection / it's not love that is crushing / it's the act of letting go / it's the past burns / razor cuts on skins / watching them walk / hearing a goodbye / that leave us tingling in our psychic powers to not believe in our ability to act lovingly / we don't love / we act lovingly / we receive loving acts / and trust in the intensity / in the affection / to be accepted / and trust in our own greatness / so I invite you in my pocket / because in there: is all the love / which is worth having / even if L E F T.

Here is what I learned about wanting.

It's a baby who feels softness wrapped in a blanket.
Comfort from rocking
A soothing in music
And ease from a cupped palm.

A toddler who enjoys bright lights and feathers
Tickles and cartoons.
At some point he learns if he doesn't get it
A scream will do.
A cry gets you what you want
A tantrum even more.
Eventually some praise, reinforcement to
Seek reward.

A child who loves music
Art
Books
And sports.

A teenager who posts
For recognition and more.
Multiple partners
And ultra-submissive
Parties.
Certificates.
And nightly kisses.
Perfect grades
For perfect scores.
Avoidance of loneliness.
Avoidance of bored . . .

Eventually an adult
Who doesn't want anymore.
Overtime not sure.
What any of this wanting is for.

H A U N T E D.
Always wanting.
It's not about wanting.
But about always wanting to be
W A N T E D.

All At Once.

You can be it all at once.
The droplets left in leaves after the rain
The rays behind the mountain tops
The soggy in your cereal
And the bow on a new gift.
The tag cut off from a brand-new top
The scratch left on old vinyl
The last percent of battery
The sugar highs from Oreos
I don't know if we are black or white
The middle or the outer sides
But I know we are the "braverous"
And we are the "smad"
The nervous and the brave
The happy and the sad.
The ending
For all bounties
Because we have no price
Every day we are free to be
Neither wrong nor right.
The first seen with open eyes
The last vision before slumber
The loss in a market
The stock on a farm
The wool in a jacket
And cuts of harm.
The drip of blood
And locks in love
How many do you count?
A song on an alter
A prayer whispered
From a mouth.

"Inseconfindence"
Say it proud
It's all we need to be
Insecure and confident.
Let humanity sing.
All at once.

ALL AT ONCE

Music is Everything.

You are an arrangement
A four-chord song
Melody
And lyrics
I hear you.
I read it.
I sense it.
And know it.
Every head turn
And note missed
You can't record this.
I can't ignore it.
It's too authentic
Underneath
The song speaks
And when I "see" you
I feel everything.

I want it back.
The moment when time is endless.
World is spinning around while standing in
Stillness.
Release because nothing seems to matter but this.
Everything matters, especially this.
Because music speaks
And when it hits me
I feel
E V E R Y T H I N G.

Eternity.

Maybe she likes to live in the chaos
Finds lust in things like
Pixie dust
And treasures in
Golden rust
Love
In whispers
That pronounce
H U S H.

Because in the quiet
There are purring kittens
And cute little mittens
Holes in overworn socks
And seconds slip on ticking clocks
Soft radiator humming
Beats of rhythmic drumming
Hugging bears
And creaks from chairs
Fully eaten mush
And strays in the brush
In the whispers that pronounce
H U S H.

Wait for the neon lights
And colors
The sound of noon
The classic reading of
"G O O D N I G H T   M O O N."

So maybe we can risk this sleep
Because normal feels like forever
A never-ending oblivion in too much certainty.
It's so much better to live in the between
Between the end and never ending,
The chaos of living.
She could strike a match and blow up
E T E R N I T Y.

Flock of birds.

When I see a hundred birds,
I wonder what they say
It looks like they all trust
The one up front to lead the way
I put trust in little things
Although I second guess
I am turning around but not
Going fully back.
I was so wrong before
But now I know I'm right.
The signs are written in the
S T A R S.
C L O U D S.
C L O C K S.
S O N G S.
And most importantly
E Y E S.

Stay.

Imagine what it would feel like
To capture these below things
To no longer just be in our minds
To get to relive the memories.

The seconds before an affectionate hug
Or breaking into genuine laugh
Finding you were right all along
Yet you thought you didn't pass.

Someone who offers help
When you feel all alone.
The name of t h a t 'person'
Showing up on your phone.

That song from forever ago
Coming on your playlist.
Meeting your idol, mentor
Or someone really famous.

Dancing in the mirror.
Singing in the shower.
Holding hands for seconds longer.
The return of lost power.

Watching a child or pet
Rest peacefully in your lap.
Coming home from a long day
And getting to take a nap.

Being on time despite traffic
The seconds of relief.
Getting your voice back
After not being able to speak.

Taste of favorite food.
Travel in good weather.
So in the moment,
Losing time all together.

Saying the truth
And it being well received
Sharing real connections
With truth and honesty.

The seconds just before
Breath and heartbeat fast
Saying I love you
And the person saying it back.

We often replay these
Because they are beautiful
And unique
They can also bring about pain
And make us feel weak.

So I caught them all for you
I'm holding them real tight
I give them selflessly
To everyone who reads them tonight.

S T A Y with this for hours.

Release.

Just because this is small
Doesn't mean it can't be loud
Scream it over rooftops . . .
Leave you raw
R E L E A S E

When you've slept for 20+ hours
Leftovers and empty bottles
From the back of your mouth
Smoke that drifts
R E L E A S E

Who are you kidding
Unfollowed and faking
Pictures and pages
Written advertising
R E L E A S E

Bodies swimming
Heated blankets
Lots of distance
Even when proximity
Is inches
R E L E A S E

You are the bee sting that never went away.

The swelling, the itch, and the pain.
That first pinch
And the last drain.
What oozes out
Yet still remains
Constant tingling
And ringing in my brain.
The sting that shivers
And quivers
All through my veins.
It's swollen, red,
And utterly insane.
I can't think of anything
Except the name. . . .
The name of the bee
That left me with nothing
But venom
And this sting site
S T A I N.

Everything Happens for a Reason.

Everything happens for a reason.
But hate when I don't know.
Control the moments to be
To force an outcome.
Persuasion
Manipulation
Gaslight flames of insanity.
So confined to beliefs
Polarized on S T R I N G S.

Do you ever feel like falling?
Do you ever want to be free?
To soar
Instead of force
Persuasion
Manipulation
Gaslight flames
Of insanity.
Polarized on strings.
Stop listening
Repeating . . .
Do you ever want to be free?
Do you ever feel like flying?
Do you ever want to make your own wings?

Winds of Change.

I jump into a pond of words,
Looking for magic.

I hope my words startle.
I hope my words cure.
I hope my words break you down
Just to build you back.

I hope my words echo.
I hope my words bark.
A melancholy way to say
I am no marker,
But gosh did you leave a mark.

It's strange how you have a way
Of moving me like that.
No words.
Fill this space.
Please don't
D I S C O N N E C T.

Ways to scare someone away.

Be so close to someone's ideal / call it fate / leaves grow green /
question eternity / ignore bad timing / give everything / offer to
fight all demons / live in seconds of clarity / decompose as the mind
talks you out of it / still try to force it / wish so hard on falling stars
/ forget how old you are / leaves turn orange / break rules / pretend
you don't need to be taken care of / obsess / know they obsess, too
/ obsess together / want to hold each other / hold each other / hold
for minutes that feel like hours / cry because it exists / leaves start
to wither / make plans / share dreams / know you are not making
this up / it's not a dream / become their ideal / be their ideal / you
are their ideal / watch them detach / leaves crumble / feel them shut
down / cry because it leaves / try to bring them back / pretend to let
go / ache in their disappearance / T W I N G E in falling leaves

Let Me Bloom.

Trusting for too long
Let me bloom.
Waiting to blossom.
To fall into you.
Your time will come.
I don't want to fall.
I don't want to bloom.
Bloomed means it's over.
I want to grow with you.
Grow and never end.
No finished project.
Only to document.
Sounds of wonder
Curiously in sync
Leaves changing colors
Then back to green.
Every time I see you
I want it to be new,
I want every particle
To be delicate.
Warm.
True.

I want transformation,
But not transformed.
Blooming
But not bloomed.
Flourishing
But not flourished.
Because done is an ending
And I'm never finished.

I'll ink you in your favorites.
Always. Bloom. With. Me.
Never completed.
Always. in. sync.
Always
BLOOMING.

Air.

Shivering on the edge of cold.
A sunset on the brink of water.
I think I think too much
But thoughts mean less than air
A I R we breathe.
A I R we speak.
A I R we feel when we meet.
The A I R of our intimacy.

A coda: Your relationship between you and you is the most important.

Those words of poetry / you said to me / I think you need to turn them around and say them to yourself / and when you're ready / when you actually believe them / when you love yourself enough / to be the poem / then you'll be ready for me / then I'll be standing there / shoulders down / sigh of relief / in knowing / I'm not too good / or better deserving / I am exactly as is / as you are / an exact resemblance of what you see in yourself / when you look at me / I wasn't always just out of reach / on the top of some pedestal / like a butterfly you can't keep / you say "but / her / flies / away" / I say / "let be / and come back" / and each time you don't believe me / it's because you don't believe in you / and when you do / when you turn around / and actually look in my eyes / at your own reflection / and recognize that in me all you see is yourself / and how wonderful that feeling is / to adore yourself as much as you know you adore somebody else / I'll still be standing there / shoulders down / sigh of relief / this time a few steps closer / a few steps closer / a few steps closer /

I see into your aura / and / how much you think / how you block out the reminders / the reruns / the fantasy / how yet the little spark still gets in when awoken at night / when you can't sleep / strings / petals / poetry / how certain things still leave you on your toes / aching / how you call it an addiction / side note, the opposite of addiction is connection / and how dare we pathologize that kind of resonance / that background music / you turned down / that slowly comes back up when you tune out the noise of the crowds / this isn't withdrawal / the shakes / or nausea / I see / I feel / I touch / I gaze / I hear how much you crave / and to me it's the most attractive thing there is / the heart pounding / soul shaking / finger tingling / goosebumps falling down your spine at the sight / warmth / thought / dreams / keep you awake / I / keep / you / awake / and to me that's the most attractive thing there is / to know who you can and cannot make fall asleep / how astounding to be / the most attractive thing / there is / and still consider yourself unwanted.

Acknowledgments.

To those who have divinely come into my life.

You made an impact and brought these words to life.

YOU A M A Z E ME.

Amanda Baker believes that we are more authentic as our childlike selves than we are as adults. We are more likely to share our truth and live our truth as children, but who says we have to stop. Amanda is a mental health therapist, 200-hour yoga instructor, and poet from Baltimore, Maryland. She attended the University of Maryland School of Social Work and James Madison University. She is a mother of her four-year-old son, Dylan, and enjoys time in nature. Amanda has self-published a poetry collection that includes written work from her early teens into her 30s. You may find her book *ASK: A Collection of Poetry, Lyrics, and Words* on Amazon and Barnes & Noble.

Thank you for supporting independent publishing.

Yellow Arrow Publishing is a nonprofit
supporting writers that identify as women. Visit
YellowArrowPublishing.com for information on our
publications, workshops, and writing opportunities.

www.ingramcontent.com/pod-product-compliance
Lightning Source LLC
Chambersburg PA
CBHW030514130626
46549CB00007B/2992